THRIVING AMIDST TWISTS

50 Essential Lessons for Entrepreneurial Resilience

Sumegha Mehta Borar

ISBN: 9798322271949

To all the resilient entrepreneurs who have withstood the tempests of the market, embraced challenges, and pressed on through the ever-shifting landscape of business. Your courage, perseverance, and unwavering determination inspire us all. May these lessons serve as a guiding light on your path to success and fulfillment.

Table of Contents

THRIVING AMIDST TWISTS

ACKNOWLEDGMENTS

Writing Thriving Amidst Twists: 50 Essential Lessons for Entrepreneurial Resilience has been an incredible journey, and I am deeply grateful to everyone who supported me along the way.

First and foremost, I would like to thank my husband & family for their unwavering support and encouragement. Your belief in me has been my greatest source of strength.

To my friends and colleagues, thank you for your insights, feedback, and for always being there to listen. Your contributions have been invaluable.

I am also immensely grateful to my mentors and advisors, whose wisdom and guidance have shaped my entrepreneurial journey. Your lessons have been instrumental in creation of this book.

THRIVING AMIDST TWISTS

INTRODUCTION

Welcome to "Thriving Amidst Twists: 50 Essential Lessons for Entrepreneurial Resilience."

If you're holding this book, it's likely you've taken the plunge into the dynamic world of entrepreneurship. Kudos to you! You've embarked on a path brimming with unexpected moments and challenges.

Within these pages lies a wealth of knowledge, actionable advice, and motivational tales to steer you through the peaks and valleys of your business venture.

Let's be clear: entrepreneurship is not a journey for the timid. It demands bravery, resolve, and an openness to the unknown. Yet, the rewards are immense, offering the chance to forge something impactful, influence change positively, and chart your own course in life.

On this path, it's common to become engrossed in the daily grind, losing track of the overarching goals and overlooking key tenets that enable us to tackle obstacles with resilience and elegance.

This book is your ally. With insights drawn from my direct experience with entrepreneurs, as well as wisdom from renowned business figures and industry experts, I've curated fifty indispensable lessons to help you not just endure but flourish through the entrepreneurial landscape.

Rest assured, this book steers clear of dense jargon and complex theories. Consider it a companionable guide, penned in an engaging tone, to reconnect you with the innate knowledge that may slip your mind amid the hustle.

Each chapter is crafted for clarity, packed with hands-on suggestions, real-world anecdotes, and steps you can apply immediately.

No matter if you're at the outset of your entrepreneurial quest or a veteran businessperson aiming to refine your acumen, there's valuable insight here for you.

So, pour yourself a coffee, settle into your favourite nook, and let's embark on this journey together. Here's to flourishing in the face of change and constructing a business that doesn't just endure but excels despite the odds. Let's begin!

In the dance of entrepreneurship change isn't a disruption; it's the rhythm that propels us forward

CHAPTER 1: EMBRACING CHANGE

Welcome to the journey of building resilience in your entrepreneurial endeavors. In this chapter, we will explore the fundamental importance of embracing change, a skill crucial for navigating the unpredictable twists and turns of the business world. So, settle in, and let's dive in!

Lesson 1: Adaptability Is Key

Think of your business as a sailboat on a vast ocean. The winds of change can come suddenly and unexpectedly, altering your course in an instant. The key to staying afloat? Adaptability. Just like a skilled sailor adjusts the sails to navigate turbulent waters, as an entrepreneur, you must adapt to changing market trends, consumer preferences, and technological advancements.

Adaptability is not about completely changing your business model every time something shifts. It's about being flexible, open-minded, and willing to adjust your strategies to meet the demands of the ever-evolving marketplace. Remember, it's not the strongest or the smartest who survive, but those most adaptable to change.

Lesson 2: Finding Opportunities in Adversity

During challenges and setbacks lies hidden potential. Instead of viewing adversity as a roadblock, train yourself to see it as an opportunity for growth and innovation. History is filled with examples of businesses that thrived during times of crisis by pivoting their strategies and seizing new opportunities.

When faced with adversity, ask yourself: What can I learn from this situation? How can I adapt my business to meet the current needs of my customers? By reframing challenges as opportunities, you'll not only build resilience but also uncover new avenues for success.

Lesson 3: Cultivating a Growth Mindset

At the heart of resilience lies a growth mindset—the belief that your abilities and intelligence can be developed through dedication and hard work. Instead of viewing failure as a reflection of your inherent limitations, see it as a steppingstone on the path to mastery.

Embrace challenges as opportunities to learn and grow. Celebrate your progress, no matter how small, and use setbacks as motivation to keep pushing forward. Remember, success is not a destination but a journey of continuous improvement.

So, as you navigate the ever-changing landscape of entrepreneurship, remember to embrace change, find opportunities in adversity, and cultivate a growth mindset. By doing so, you'll not only weather the storms but emerge stronger and more resilient than ever before.

Together, let's embark on this expedition, possessing the vision and expertise to flourish in the entrepreneurial odyssey. To a journey filled with discovery and success.

Embracing Change: The Bezos Blueprint for Business Agility

Jeff Bezos, the founder of Amazon, is a perfect example of an entrepreneur who thrives on change. Starting with a small online bookstore in his garage, he grew Amazon into one of the biggest and most diverse tech companies in the world. This journey shows how good Bezos is at adapting and coming up with new ideas.

Bezos didn't just stick to selling books. He quickly added more products like electronics, clothes, and even streaming services. This move helped Amazon stay ahead as shopping online became more popular.

But Bezos didn't stop there. He also saw the potential in new technology. He started Amazon Web Services (AWS), a cloud computing service, in 2006. This was a smart move that helped businesses and put Amazon at the forefront of tech.

Bezos is known for changing his business to meet new customer needs and market changes. He's always looking ahead, whether it's making delivery faster or getting into the grocery business with Whole Foods. His ability to innovate has kept Amazon successful.

In short, Jeff Bezos and Amazon show how important it is to be open to change in business. By always being ready to adapt and try new things, Bezos turned Amazon from a simple bookstore into a giant in both e-commerce and tech. His success comes from being able to change with the times.

In Bezos Words

"I very frequently get the question: 'What's going to change in the next 10 years?' And that is a very interesting question; it's a very common one. I almost never get the question: 'What's not going to change in the next 10 years?' And I submit to you that that second question is the more important of the two -- because you can build a business strategy around the things that are stable in time. ... In our retail business, we know that customers want low prices, and I know that's going to be true 10 years from now. They want fast delivery; they want vast selection. It's impossible to imagine a future 10 years from now where a customer

comes up and says, 'Jeff I love Amazon; I just wish the prices were a little higher,' [or] 'I love Amazon; I just wish you'd deliver a little more slowly.' Impossible. And so, the effort we put into those things, spinning those things up, we know the energy we put into it today will still be paying off dividends for our customers 10 years from now. When you have something that you know is true, even over the long term, you can afford to put a lot of energy into it.

NOTES AND KEY TAKEAWAYS

Failure isn't a setback; it's a roadmap to success, showing us the detours, we need to take

CHAPTER 2: MANAGING FAILURE

Failure is an inevitable part of the entrepreneurial journey. It's not a matter of if you will face setbacks, but when. How you respond to failure can make all the difference in your success. In this chapter, we'll explore essential lessons for managing failure and building resilience in the face of adversity.

Lesson 4: Learning from Setbacks

Setbacks are not the end of the road; they're opportunities for growth. When things don't go as planned, take a step back and ask yourself, "What can I learn from this?" Every failure holds valuable lessons that can help you improve and succeed in the future.

Think of setbacks as feedback. They highlight areas where you can refine your approach or develop new skills. Embrace failure as a natural part of the learning process. Remember, some of the most successful entrepreneurs have faced numerous failures before achieving greatness.

Lesson 5: Resilience in the Face of Failure

Resilience is the ability to bounce back from adversity stronger than before. When faced with failure, it's normal to feel discouraged or even defeated. But it's how you respond to failure that defines your resilience.

Instead of dwelling on what went wrong, focus on what you can control. Take proactive steps to overcome obstacles and move forward. Surround yourself with a supportive network of mentors, friends, and fellow entrepreneurs who can offer encouragement and perspective.

Resilience is not about avoiding failure; it's about facing it head-on and persevering despite the odds. Remember, every successful entrepreneur has experienced their fair share of setbacks. It's your resilience that will ultimately determine your success.

Lesson 6: Using Failure as Fuel for Success

Failure is not the opposite of success; it's a steppingstone to success. Instead of letting failure hold you back, use it as fuel to propel you forward. Channel your disappointment and frustration into motivation to try again, but this time with more knowledge and determination.

Every failure brings you one step closer to success, as long as you're willing to keep pushing forward. Embrace failure as a necessary part of the journey and celebrate the lessons learned along the way. Remember, the path to success is rarely linear. It's the twists and turns, the ups and downs, that make the journey worthwhile.

In conclusion, managing failure is not about avoiding it altogether but learning to navigate it with resilience and determination. Embrace failure as an opportunity for growth, and let it fuel your drive to succeed. With the right mindset and support system, you can turn setbacks into steppingstones on your entrepreneurial journey.

Sara Blakely's Spanx Story: Turning Setbacks into Success

Sara Blakely's entrepreneurial journey with Spanx exemplifies the art of managing failure with grace and resilience. As the founder of Spanx, a company that revolutionized the shapewear industry, Blakely faced numerous obstacles and setbacks along the way. However, her ability to navigate through failure ultimately led to the creation of a multi-million-dollar business empire.

Blakely's journey began with a simple idea: to create comfortable and effective shapewear that women could wear under their clothing. Armed with this vision, she poured her savings into developing the product and securing manufacturing, only to face rejection after rejection from potential investors and retailers. Despite these setbacks, Blakely refused to give up on her dream.

Instead of allowing failure to deter her, Blakely used each rejection as an opportunity for growth and learning. She embraced feedback, refined her product, and persisted in her pursuit of success. Blakely's resilience was evident in her willingness to adapt and innovate, even in the face of adversity.

Eventually, Blakely's perseverance paid off when she secured a meeting with a buyer from a major department store who agreed to carry Spanx. From there, the brand gained momentum, quickly becoming a household name, and revolutionizing the shapewear industry.

Blakely's story serves as a powerful reminder that failure is not the end of the road but rather a steppingstone on the path to success. If you learn from your mistakes and keep going, you can get past any problem and make your dreams come true. Sara Blakely's ability to stay strong in tough times shows us all how powerful it is to keep going and believe in ourselves.

In Sara's words

I think failure is nothing more than life's way of nudging you that you are off course. My attitude to failure is not attached to outcome, but in not trying. It is liberating. Most people attach failure to something not working out or how people perceive you. This way, it is about answering yourself.

Don't be intimidated by what you don't know. That can be your greatest strength and ensure that you do things differently from everyone else.

NOTES AND KEY TAKEAWAYS

NOTES AND KEY TAKEAWAYS

In the journey of entrepreneurship, our network isn't just our safety net; it's our trampoline, propelling us to new heights

CHAPTER 3: BUILDING A SUPPORT NETWORK

Welcome to the third chapter of our exploration into the heart of entrepreneurial resilience. In this chapter, we delve deep into a fundamental element of enduring success—the creation and nurturing of a robust support network. This network, often an amalgamation of mentors, peers, friends, and family, serves as the backbone of your entrepreneurial endeavors.

Whether you are taking your first tentative steps into the business world or are a seasoned player, the company you keep can significantly influence your path. A strong support network provides more than just advice; it offers a safety net during times of uncertainty, a sounding board for your ideas, and a cheering squad for your victories.

As we journey through this chapter, we'll uncover the strategies for building a circle of allies who believe in your vision, challenge you to grow, and stand by you when the going gets tough. We'll learn how to identify the right individuals who will add value to your journey and how to cultivate these relationships into lasting partnerships.

Embrace the wisdom that you don't have to go it alone. The right support can be the wind in your sails, propelling you forward even when the waters are choppy. Let's embark on this vital aspect of your entrepreneurial voyage and discover how a solid support network can be your greatest asset on the road to resilience and success.

Lesson 7: Importance of Mentorship

Let's kick things off by talking about mentorship. A mentor is your guide through the business wilderness, someone who's already faced the challenges you're encountering and can share valuable lessons from their own journey.

Having a mentor can help you navigate the ups and downs of entrepreneurship, avoid common pitfalls, and stay focused on your goals.

Finding a mentor doesn't have to be complicated. Reach out to people in your industry who you admire and respect. Don't be afraid to ask for help or guidance – most successful entrepreneurs are more than willing to share their knowledge with others.

As you seek out a mentor, prioritize these traits:

1. Experience: They should have a track record of success and experience in your field.

2. Communication: A good mentor communicates clearly and effectively, offering advice that's easy to understand and apply.

3. Commitment: They should be genuinely interested in helping you succeed and willing to invest time in your development.

4. Honesty: Look for someone who will give you straightforward feedback, even when it's tough to hear.

5. Respect: Your mentor should respect you and your vision, supporting you in your goals.

Finding the right mentor involves reaching out to professionals you admire. And remember, a successful mentorship involves mutual respect and appreciation—value their time and wisdom, and your journey together will be even more rewarding.

Lesson 8: Surrounding yourself with the Right People

Next up, let's talk about the importance of surrounding yourself with the right people. As the saying goes, "You are the average of the five people you spend the most time with." Surround yourself with positive, motivated individuals who inspire you to be your best self.

This doesn't just apply to your professional life – it's equally important in your personal life as well. Surround yourself with friends and family who support your entrepreneurial endeavors and lift you up when you're feeling down. And don't be afraid to distance yourself from negative influences – sometimes, you have to let go of toxic relationships in order to thrive.

Lesson 9: Leveraging Networks for Growth

Finally, let's talk about the power of networking. Building a strong network of contacts can open countless opportunities for growth and collaboration. Attend industry events, join online communities, and don't be afraid to put yourself out there.

But networking isn't just about collecting business cards – it's about building genuine, meaningful relationships with people who share your passions and values. Take the time to get to know others on a personal level, and always look for ways to add value to your network. Remember, you never know when a casual conversation or chance encounter could lead to your next big opportunity.

And so, we've uncovered three pivotal lessons to fortify your entrepreneurial journey. Whether it's the wisdom of a mentor, the energy of a positive circle, or the opportunities within an expanded network, the significance of a strong support system cannot be overstressed. It's the collective strength of these relationships that can propel you forward through the unpredictable journey of entrepreneurship. Remember, the triumphs of business are most fulfilling when celebrated with those who have supported you along the way. Embrace the collective spirit, and let it guide you to shared success.

Bill Gates: Co-founder of Microsoft

In Chapter 3, "Building a Support Network," we delve into the crucial role of mentors, advisors, and collaborators in an entrepreneur's journey to success. Bill Gates, the co-founder of Microsoft, serves as an exemplary case study in understanding the significance of building a robust support network.

Bill Gates recognized early in his career that success in the highly competitive world of technology required more than just technical expertise; it demanded strategic guidance, mentorship, and a network of trusted advisors. Gates understood the value of learning from those who had already achieved success in their respective fields, and he actively sought out mentors who could offer invaluable insights and advice.

One of Gates's most notable mentors was Warren Buffett, the renowned investor and chairman of Berkshire Hathaway. Gates admired Buffett's business acumen and investment philosophy, and he sought his guidance on various strategic decisions throughout his career. Buffett's wisdom and mentorship played a crucial role in shaping Gates's approach to business and investment, particularly during Microsoft's early years of growth and expansion.

In addition to seeking mentorship from established industry leaders, Gates also recognized the importance of surrounding himself with talented and like-minded individuals who shared his vision and passion for technology. One such individual was Paul Allen, Gates's childhood friend and co-founder of Microsoft. Together, Gates and Allen forged a formidable partnership, complementing each other's strengths and driving Microsoft's innovation and success.

Gates leveraged his network of mentors, advisors, and collaborators to navigate the challenges of building a tech startup and capitalize on emerging opportunities in the rapidly evolving industry. Whether it was seeking advice on strategic partnerships, navigating regulatory hurdles, or recruiting top talent, Gates relied on his support network to overcome obstacles and propel Microsoft to become a global tech powerhouse.

Ultimately, Gates's ability to build and leverage a strong support network was instrumental in Microsoft's success, demonstrating the power of collaboration, mentorship, and strategic networking in the journey of entrepreneurship. His story serves as a compelling example of how entrepreneurs can harness the collective wisdom and support of their network to achieve their goals and aspirations.

NOTES AND KEY TAKEAWAYS

Amidst the chaos of entrepreneurship, remember: self-care isn't selfish; it's the fuel that keeps our engine running.

CHAPTER 4: SELF-CARE AND WELL-BEING

In this chapter, we'll dive into the crucial topic of self-care and well-being. As entrepreneurs, it's easy to get caught up in the hustle and bustle of building our businesses, but it's essential to remember that taking care of ourselves is just as important as taking care of our ventures.

Lesson 10: Prioritizing Mental Health

Let's start with a topic that's often overlooked in the entrepreneurial world: mental health. The pressures of running a business can weigh heavily on one's psyche, making it crucial to place mental well-being at the forefront of our priorities. Ignoring mental health is akin to neglecting a wound—it only worsens with time.

It's imperative to conduct regular mental check-ups. Pause and reflect: How are you really feeling? Are the burdens of stress, anxiety, or the specter of burnout looming over you? Recognize these signs and act promptly. Support is within reach and comes in various forms—professional therapy, mindfulness practices like meditation, or heartfelt conversations with friends or mentors. These avenues of support are not just lifelines; they are the building blocks for sustained success and contentment.

You're in good company on this path. Many entrepreneurs face similar battles with mental health, and it's important to remember that reaching out is a testament to your strength, not a surrender to weakness. By giving mental health the attention it deserves, you equip yourself with the resilience and poise needed to navigate the ebbs and flows of the entrepreneurial world. Let's embrace this chapter with the understanding that caring for the mind is as essential as any business strategy we deploy.

Lesson 11: Maintaining Work-Life Balance

Next up, let's talk about work-life balance—or as some like to call it, work-life integration. As entrepreneurs, it's easy to fall into the trap of working around the clock, sacrificing our personal lives for the sake of our businesses. But here's the truth: burnout is real, and it's a surefire way to sabotage your success.

Finding a healthy balance between work and life is essential for your well-being and the success of your business. Set boundaries around your work hours and stick to them as much as possible. Make time for activities that bring you joy and fulfillment outside of work, whether it's spending time with loved ones, pursuing hobbies, or simply taking a walk-in nature.

Remember, you're in this for the long haul, and sustainable success requires taking care of yourself along the way. By prioritizing work-life balance, you'll not only prevent burnout but also foster greater creativity, productivity, and overall happiness in both your personal and professional life.

Lesson 12: Finding Joy in the Journey

Finally, let's talk about finding joy in the journey of entrepreneurship. Building a business is undoubtedly challenging, but it's also incredibly rewarding. Don't forget to celebrate your wins, no matter how small, and savor the moments of progress and growth along the way.

Take time to reflect on why you started this journey in the first place. What are your passions, values, and goals? Connect with your purpose and let it fuel your drive and determination. Remember, success is not just about reaching the destination; it's about enjoying the ride and embracing the lessons learned along the way.

So, as you navigate the twists and turns of entrepreneurship, don't forget to prioritize your mental health, maintain a healthy work-life balance, and find joy in the journey. By taking care of yourself, you'll not only become a more resilient entrepreneur but also lead a more fulfilling and purpose-driven life.

Keep thriving amidst twists and remember—you've got this!

Arianna Huffington: Co-founder of the Huffington Post

Arianna Huffington, the co-founder of The Huffington Post, is a prominent advocate for self-care and well-being in the workplace. Her personal journey serves as a powerful case study illustrating the significance of prioritizing self-care, especially in high-stress environments like entrepreneurship.

Huffington's dedication to her work and relentless pursuit of success eventually led to a critical turning point in her life – burnout. After collapsing from exhaustion and sleep deprivation in 2007, Huffington realized the detrimental impact of neglecting her well-being. This wake-up call prompted her to reassess her priorities and make significant changes in her approach to work and life.

Recognizing the importance of self-care not just for herself but also for her team, Huffington took decisive action to integrate well-being practices into the culture of The Huffington Post. She introduced innovative initiatives such as nap rooms, meditation spaces, and wellness programs aimed at promoting work-life balance and reducing stress among employees.

By encouraging her team to prioritize self-care, Huffington fostered a positive and supportive work environment where employees felt valued and empowered to take care of their physical and mental health. This, in turn, led to increased productivity, creativity, and overall job satisfaction within the organization.

Huffington's commitment to self-care not only transformed her own life but also set a powerful example for leaders in all industries. Through her advocacy, she has helped shift the narrative around success to emphasize the importance of holistic well-being.

In conclusion, Arianna Huffington's journey with The Huffington Post serves as a compelling case study on the transformative power of self-care and well-being in the workplace. By prioritizing self-care and implementing supportive policies, Huffington not only improved her own health but also created a culture of wellness that positively impacted the lives of her employees. Her story reminds us that self-care is not a luxury but a necessity for sustainable success and fulfillment in both work and life.

NOTES AND KEY TAKEAWAYS

NOTES AND KEY TAKEAWAYS

In the face of adversity, persistence isn't stubbornness; it's the unwavering belief in our purpose that keeps us moving forward.

CHAPTER 5: DEVELOPING PERSISTANCE

In this chapter, we're diving into a crucial aspect of resilience: persistence. It's the fuel that keeps your entrepreneurial engine running, even when the road gets rough. So, let's strap in and explore the power of perseverance, staying committed to your vision, and overcoming obstacles with grit.

Lesson 13: The Power of Perseverance

Perseverance is like that old friend who sticks around no matter what. It's about refusing to give up, even when the odds seem stacked against you. Remember those late nights spent troubleshooting a problem or those moments when it felt like success was just out of reach? That's perseverance in action. It's about pushing through the tough times because you know that success lies on the other side.

Picture this: you've hit a roadblock. Maybe your latest product didn't take off as expected, or perhaps you faced rejection after rejection from potential investors. It's easy to feel defeated, isn't it? But here's the thing – every successful entrepreneur faces setbacks. The key is in how you respond to them.

Remember, it's not about avoiding failure; it's about bouncing back from it. Perseverance is that inner fire that keeps you going, even when everything seems to be working against you. It's about picking yourself up, dusting yourself off, and getting back in the game.

Think of your favorite success story – whether it's Elon Musk, Oprah Winfrey, or Steve Jobs. They all faced countless obstacles on their journey to success. But what set them apart was their unwavering perseverance. So, the next time you face a setback, remember, it's not the end of the road; it's just a detour on the path to success.

Lesson 14: Staying Committed to your Vision.

Now, let's talk about vision. As an entrepreneur, you have a vision – a dream of what you want to achieve. But here's the thing about dreams: they require commitment. It's easy to get distracted by shiny objects or swayed by the latest trends, but staying true to your vision is what will ultimately lead you to success.

Think about why you started this journey in the first place. What is it that drives you? What impact do you want to make in the world?

Keep that vision front and center, and let it guide you through the ups and downs of entrepreneurship.

Sure, there will be days when you question whether it's all worth it. But trust me, it is. Stay committed to your vision, even when it feels like the whole world is against you. Because in the end, it's your unwavering commitment that will set you apart from the rest.

Lesson 15: Overcoming Obstacles with Grit

Lastly, let's talk about grit. Angela Duckworth, a psychologist, and researcher, defines grit as "perseverance and passion for long-term goals." In other words, it's about having the resilience to keep going, even when the going gets tough.

Grit is what separates the dreamers from the doers. It's that inner strength that allows you to push through adversity and come out stronger on the other side.

So, how do you develop grit? It's simple – by facing challenges head-on and refusing to back down.

Every obstacle you encounter is an opportunity to build your grit muscle. Embrace challenges as opportunities for growth and remember that failure is not the end – it's just another step on the path to success.

In conclusion, developing persistence is essential for entrepreneurial success. Whether it's persevering through setbacks, staying committed to your vision, or overcoming obstacles with grit, remember that resilience is not just about bouncing back – it's about bouncing forward. So, keep pushing forward, stay true to your vision, and never lose sight of the incredible impact you're capable of making.

Elon Musk: CEO of SpaceX and Tesla

Elon Musk, the visionary CEO of SpaceX, and Tesla, embodies the epitome of relentless persistence in entrepreneurship. Throughout his career, Musk has faced numerous setbacks, challenges, and even criticism, yet his unwavering commitment to his bold visions has been unwavering.

One of Musk's most notable ventures, SpaceX, was born out of his desire to revolutionize space exploration. In the early days of SpaceX, Musk encountered skepticism from industry experts and faced daunting technical challenges. However, he persisted, pouring his own fortune into the company, and refusing to give up on his dream of making space travel more accessible and affordable. Despite multiple failed rocket launches and setbacks, Musk continued to push forward, learning from each failure, and iterating on his designs.

Musk's persistence paid off when SpaceX achieved its first successful orbital launch in 2008, becoming the first privately funded company to do so. Since then, SpaceX has made history multiple times, with milestones such as launching the Falcon Heavy, landing, and reusing rocket boosters, and transporting astronauts to the International Space Station. Musk's relentless pursuit of his vision has not only transformed the space industry but has also inspired a new generation of space enthusiasts and entrepreneurs.

In addition to SpaceX, Musk's other venture, Tesla, has also faced its fair share of challenges. From production delays to financial difficulties, Tesla has weathered numerous storms on its journey to revolutionize the automotive industry with electric vehicles. Despite facing skepticism from traditional automakers and Wall Street analysts, Musk remained steadfast in his commitment to accelerating the world's transition to sustainable energy.

Musk's persistence and determination have been evident in Tesla's continued innovation and growth. Under his leadership, Tesla has achieved significant milestones, including the successful launch of mass-market electric vehicles like the Model S, Model 3, and Model Y, as well as advancements in battery technology and autonomous driving. Despite facing setbacks and naysayers, Musk's unwavering belief in his vision has propelled Tesla to become one of the most valuable automakers in the world.

Elon Musk's story serves as a powerful reminder of the importance of persistence in entrepreneurship. Despite facing numerous challenges and setbacks, Musk remained committed to his vision, refusing to let obstacles stand in the way of his goals. His relentless pursuit of innovation and audacious goals has not only transformed industries but has also inspired countless entrepreneurs to dream big and never give up on their visions. Elon Musk's journey with SpaceX and Tesla showcases the incredible power of persistence in achieving entrepreneurial success.

NOTES AND KEY TAKEAWAYS

NOTES AND KEY TAKEAWAYS

Entrepreneurship is a game of chess, not checkers; every move counts, and strategic decisions are the key to victory.

CHAPTER 6: STRATEGIC DECISION MAKING

In this chapter, we'll delve into the art of strategic decision making. As entrepreneurs, we often find ourselves faced with tough choices, especially when the pressure is on. But fear not! I'm here to equip you with the tools and insights you need to navigate these challenges with confidence.

Lesson 16: Making Decisions Under Pressure

Picture this: you're faced with a high-stakes decision, deadlines looming, and the pressure is on. It's moments like these that truly test your ability to think clearly and make sound decisions.

First off, take a deep breath. Seriously, do it. When the pressure's on, it's easy to let stress cloud your judgment. So, pause, gather your thoughts, and assess the situation calmly.

Next, gather information. Make sure you have all the facts and figures you need to make an informed decision. Consult with your team, mentors, or trusted advisors if necessary. Remember, you don't have to go it alone.

Now, weigh your options. Consider the potential risks and rewards of each course of action. And don't forget to trust your gut – intuition can be a powerful guide in times of uncertainty.

Finally, act. Make the call and commit to your decision wholeheartedly. Remember, indecision is often worse than making the wrong decision. Embrace the opportunity to learn and grow from whatever outcome arises.

Lesson 17: Risk Management and Mitigation

Ah, risk – the unavoidable companion of entrepreneurship. But here's the thing: risk isn't necessarily a bad thing. It's all about how you manage it.

Start by identifying potential risks. What could go wrong? And more importantly, what can you do to minimize those risks?

Next, develop a risk management plan. Put measures in place to mitigate potential threats to your business.

Whether it's investing in cybersecurity, diversifying your revenue streams, or securing insurance, proactive risk management can save you a world of trouble down the line.

But remember, risk is also synonymous with opportunity. Don't be afraid to take calculated risks in pursuit of your goals. Just make sure you're prepared for whatever curveballs may come your way.

Lesson 18: Learning to Pivot when Necessary.

In business, as in life, things don't always go according to plan. And that's okay. In fact, it's often those unexpected twists and turns that lead to the greatest breakthroughs.

So, when the winds of change come knocking, don't resist. Embrace the opportunity to pivot – to shift course in pursuit of new opportunities or to better align with evolving market demands.

But here's the key: pivot with purpose. Don't just change for the sake of change. Take the time to reassess your goals, your market, and your resources. And then pivot with intention, confident in your ability to adapt and thrive in the face of uncertainty.

Remember, resilience isn't about avoiding challenges – it's about embracing them head-on and emerging stronger on the other side. So, embrace the journey, and never stop learning, growing, and pivoting towards success.

Reed Hastings: Co-Founder of Netflix

Reed Hastings, the co-founder of Netflix, exemplifies strategic decision-making through his visionary leadership and bold moves that transformed the company from a DVD rental service into a streaming powerhouse.

At the turn of the millennium, Netflix disrupted the traditional video rental market by offering DVD rentals through mail-order subscriptions, challenging the dominance of brick-and-mortar rental stores like Blockbuster. However, Hastings recognized early on the growing shift in consumer preferences towards digital content delivery and the potential of streaming technology.

In 2007, Hastings made a pivotal decision to launch Netflix's streaming service, despite skepticism from industry insiders and existing investors. He foresaw the convergence of broadband internet access and digital entertainment, betting on the future of streaming as the primary mode of content consumption.

Hastings's strategic foresight was evident in Netflix's investment in original content production. Recognizing the importance of exclusive and compelling content to attract and retain subscribers, Netflix began producing its own original series and movies, such as "House of Cards" and "Stranger Things." This move not only differentiated Netflix from competitors but also reduced its reliance on licensing deals with traditional studios.

Moreover, Hastings demonstrated strategic agility by pivoting Netflix's business model to focus primarily on streaming, gradually phasing out its DVD rental service. This strategic shift allowed Netflix to capitalize on the growing demand for on-demand, anytime, anywhere entertainment, while also reducing operational complexities and costs associated with physical distribution.

As a result of Hastings's strategic decision-making, Netflix emerged as a global entertainment leader, revolutionizing the way people consume media. Today, Netflix boasts millions of subscribers worldwide and has become synonymous with binge-watching and original content production. Hastings's bold and forward-thinking approach to strategic decision-making has cemented Netflix's position as a dominant force in the entertainment industry and serves as a testament to the power of visionary leadership in driving business transformation.

NOTES AND KEY TAKEAWAYS

NOTES AND KEY TAKEAWAYS

In the stormy seas of business, financial wisdom isn't just a life raft; it's the compass that guides us to calmer waters

CHAPTER 7: FINANCIAL RESILIENCE

Welcome to the financial resilience zone. In this chapter, we're going to dive into the nitty-gritty of handling your finances like a pro. Don't worry; we'll keep it light, practical, and packed with tips you can use right away.

Lesson 19: Managing Cash Flow Effectively

Let's start with the lifeblood of your business: cash flow. Picture it like the oxygen that keeps you breathing. Without it, things can get pretty suffocating, right? Managing cash flow effectively means ensuring you have enough money coming in to cover your expenses, especially during those inevitable slow seasons.

First things first, track your cash flow religiously. Know what's coming in and what's going out. It sounds basic, but you'd be surprised how many entrepreneurs overlook this simple step. Use tools like spreadsheets or accounting software to stay on top of it.

Next up, keep an eye on your invoicing. Send invoices promptly and follow up on overdue payments. Remember, you're not a charity; you deserve to be paid for your hard work.

Lastly, build a buffer. Set aside some cash for emergencies or unexpected expenses. It's like having a safety net to catch you if you stumble. Trust me; you'll thank yourself later.

Lesson 20: Building Financial Cushions

Speaking of safety nets, let's talk about building financial cushions. Think of it as your rainy-day fund, ready to shield you from storms that might come your way.

Start by setting savings goals. Aim to stash away a certain percentage of your revenue each month. It might not seem like much at first, but over time, those pennies add up.

Cut unnecessary expenses. Do you really need that fancy office space or those daily lattes? Trim the fat and redirect those funds into your savings. And don't forget about debt. Pay it off as quickly as you can to free up more cash for your cushion.

The less you owe, the more secure you'll feel.

Lesson 21: Diversifying Revenue Streams.

Now, let's talk about spreading your wings and diversifying your revenue streams. Relying on a single income source is like putting all your eggs in one basket. If that basket drops, well, you know the rest.

Explore new opportunities. Can you offer additional products or services that complement what you're already doing? Think outside the box and find ways to expand your offerings.
Tap into different markets. Don't limit yourself to just one demographic or industry.

Cast a wider net and see what other fish you can catch.

And don't forget about passive income. Whether it's through investments, royalties, or affiliate marketing, find ways to make money while you sleep. It's like having your own personal ATM.
Alright, that wraps up our financial resilience crash course. Remember, managing cash flow, building financial cushions, and diversifying revenue streams are all essential ingredients for a healthy, thriving business.

So go ahead, put these lessons into action, and watch your business soar to new heights!

Warren Buffet: Chairman and CEO of Berkshire Hathaway

Warren Buffett, widely regarded as one of the greatest investors of all time, epitomizes financial resilience through his unparalleled long-term investment strategy and disciplined approach to managing Berkshire Hathaway's vast portfolio. Buffett's journey towards financial resilience is a testament to his unwavering commitment to sound investment principles and his ability to navigate through various market cycles with confidence and foresight

Throughout his illustrious career, Buffett has demonstrated an acute understanding of the fundamental principles of investing. He focuses on high-quality businesses with strong fundamentals, seeking companies with durable competitive advantages, competent management teams, and attractive long-term prospects. Buffett's emphasis on investing in businesses with intrinsic value and sustainable competitive advantages has enabled Berkshire Hathaway to weather market fluctuations and economic downturns with resilience.

Buffett's prudent financial management extends beyond stock selection to encompass a disciplined approach to risk management and capital allocation. He avoids speculative investments and complex financial instruments, preferring instead to invest in businesses that he can understand and evaluate based on their underlying fundamentals. Buffett's emphasis on preserving capital and managing risk has enabled Berkshire Hathaway to maintain a strong financial position even during challenging times.

One of Buffett's most notable qualities is his patience and long-term perspective. He famously quips, "Our favourite holding period is forever," emphasizing his commitment to holding investments for the long term. Buffett's ability to resist the temptation of short-term market fluctuations and focus on the intrinsic value of businesses has contributed to Berkshire Hathaway's consistent returns and sustained growth over the decades.

Furthermore, Buffett's transparency and integrity in his dealings with shareholders and stakeholders have earned him the trust and respect of investors worldwide. His annual letters to shareholders provide invaluable insights into his investment philosophy, strategy, and decision-making process, fostering transparency and accountability within Berkshire Hathaway.

In summary, Warren Buffett's financial resilience stems from his unwavering adherence to sound investment principles, disciplined risk management, patience, and long-term perspective. His ability to focus on high-quality businesses with strong fundamentals, coupled with his prudent financial management, has enabled Berkshire Hathaway to navigate through various market cycles and economic challenges with resilience. Buffett's legacy serves as a beacon of inspiration for investors seeking to build enduring wealth through disciplined investing and financial resilience.

NOTES AND KEY TAKEAWAYS

NOTES AND KEY TAKEAWAYS

A resilient team isn’t just a collection of individuals; it’s a family that weathers the storms together and emerges stronger than ever

CHAPTER 8: BUILDING A RESILIENT TEAM

Welcome to the financial resilience zone. In this chapter, we're going to dive into the nitty-gritty of handling your finances like a pro. Don't worry; we'll keep it light, practical, and packed with tips you can use right away. Welcome to the heart of your entrepreneurial journey – your team. They're not just colleagues; they're the backbone of your venture, the ones who will stand by your side through thick and thin. In this chapter, we'll delve into how to foster a resilient culture within your team, communicate effectively during challenging times, and support each other through the inevitable hurdles.

Lesson 22: Fostering a Culture of Resilience

Imagine your team as the backbone of your business. Just like how a strong spine supports the body, a resilient team supports your venture through thick and thin. But how do you cultivate this culture of resilience within your team?

It starts with you, the leader. Be transparent about the challenges ahead and encourage open communication. Picture this: your team as a tight-knit community, where everyone feels valued, supported, and empowered to take risks.

That's the essence of a resilient culture. It starts with you, the leader. Lead by example, showing vulnerability, embracing failure, and bouncing back stronger. Encourage open communication, where ideas flow freely, and mistakes are viewed as learning opportunities. Celebrate resilience, recognizing and rewarding team members who demonstrate it. Together, cultivate an environment where resilience isn't just a buzzword but a way of life.

Embrace failures as learning opportunities and celebrate successes, no matter how small. Encourage creativity and innovation, and most importantly, lead by example. When your team sees you embracing resilience, they'll follow suit.

Lesson 23: Effective Communication in Times of Crises

When the going gets tough, communication becomes more critical than ever. Your team looks to you for guidance and reassurance. Be transparent about the challenges you're facing and the strategies you're implementing to overcome them. Listen actively to their concerns and ideas, fostering a sense of unity and collaboration. Keep channels of communication open, whether it's through regular team meetings, one-on-one check-ins, or virtual platforms.

Be clear in your communication, provide direction, and instill confidence in your team's ability to overcome obstacles together. Remember, a unified team is a resilient team.

Remember, it's not just about what you say but how you say it – with empathy, clarity, and honesty.

Lesson 24: Supporting Team members with Challenges.

As an entrepreneur, you're not just a leader; you're also a mentor and a support system for your team members. When they face challenges, it's your role to be there for them, offering guidance, encouragement, and practical support.

Listen to their concerns, provide constructive feedback, and empower them to find solutions. Recognize their efforts and celebrate their resilience. By supporting your team members through challenges, you not only foster a culture of resilience but also strengthen the bond within your team.

Your team is your greatest asset, and their well-being is paramount. During difficult times, offer unwavering support to each team member. Check in regularly, asking how they're doing both personally and professionally. Provide resources and opportunities for growth, whether it's through training programs, mentorship, or mental health initiatives. Encourage a healthy work-life balance, recognizing the importance of rest and recharge. And above all, be there for them – as a leader, as a mentor, and as a friend.

Remember, building a resilient team isn't just about weathering the storm – it's about thriving amidst the twists and turns of entrepreneurship. By fostering a culture of resilience, communicating effectively, and supporting each other through challenges, you'll not only strengthen your team but also propel your venture to new heights. Together, you can conquer any obstacle that comes your way.

Keep Inspiring & Keep Leading.

Sheryl Sandberg: COO of Facebook

In the realm of building resilient teams, few examples shine as brightly as the case of Sheryl Sandberg, the Chief Operating Officer of Facebook. Throughout her tenure, Sandberg demonstrated a remarkable ability to foster a culture of openness, collaboration, and support within the company.

At Facebook, Sandberg recognized that a resilient team is not just about individual talents but about how those talents come together to support and uplift one another. She emphasized the importance of transparency and communication, encouraging team members to share their ideas, concerns, and feedback openly.

One of the key aspects of Sandberg's leadership was her belief in empowering employees to take ownership of their work and contribute meaningfully to the company's goals. By providing a platform for voices to be heard and ideas to be valued, she created an environment where team members felt empowered to innovate and take calculated risks.

During times of crisis, such as data breaches or public scrutiny, Sandberg's leadership was instrumental in guiding the team through challenges with resilience and grace. Rather than shying away from difficult conversations, she encouraged honest dialogue and collaboration to address issues head-on.

Sandberg's commitment to building a resilient team at Facebook has proven invaluable, particularly in navigating the complexities of the digital landscape. By fostering a culture of trust, respect, and support, she has helped Facebook weather storms and emerge stronger, highlighting the indispensable role of a resilient team in achieving sustained success in today's fast-paced world.

NOTES AND KEY TAKEAWAYS

NOTES AND KEY TAKEAWAYS

Innovation isn't just about thinking outside the box; it's about realizing there is no box and embracing the infinite possibilities that lie beyond

CHAPTER 9: EMBRACING INNOVATION

Welcome to the world of innovation, where resilience and creativity collide to create something truly remarkable. In this chapter, we're going to dive into the exciting realm of innovation and explore how it can be your secret weapon in building resilience for your entrepreneurial journey. So, buckle up and let's embark on this exhilarating ride together!

Lesson 25: The Role of Innovation in Resilience

Let's start by understanding why innovation is so crucial for resilience. Think of your business as a ship sailing through rough seas. Without innovation, you're like a ship with no compass, no way to navigate through storms and find new opportunities. Innovation is your compass, guiding you toward smoother waters and helping you adapt to whatever challenges come your way. Innovation isn't just about coming up with groundbreaking ideas or inventing the next big thing (though that's pretty cool too).

It's about constantly seeking ways to improve, evolve, and stay relevant in a rapidly changing world. Whether it's finding more efficient processes, creating new products or services, or reimagining your business model, innovation is what keeps your business moving forward.

Lesson 26: Embracing Change and Innovation

Now, let's talk about embracing change and innovation. Change can be scary, we get it. Stepping out of your comfort zone and trying something new can feel like jumping off a cliff without a parachute. But here's the thing: change is inevitable. And instead of fearing it, why not embrace it?

Think of change as an opportunity for growth. Every time you try something new, you're expanding your horizons, pushing your boundaries, and learning valuable lessons along the way. Embrace change with open arms, and you'll be amazed at how much you can achieve.

And remember, innovation isn't just about big, flashy ideas. It's about making small, incremental changes that add up over time. So don't be afraid to experiment, to try new things, and to fail. Because with every failure comes an opportunity to learn, to grow, and to come back stronger than ever before.

Lesson 27: Staying Ahead of the Curve

In today's hyper-competitive landscape, staying ahead of the curve is more important than ever. But how do you do it? Simple: by constantly innovating and pushing the boundaries of what's possible.

Keep your finger on the pulse of industry trends, listen to your customers, and always be on the lookout for new opportunities. Don't wait for change to happen—be the change!

Whether it's investing in new technologies, experimenting with new business models, or fostering a culture of innovation within your team, staying ahead of the curve is all about staying one step ahead of the competition.

So how do you stay ahead of the curve? By staying curious, by staying hungry, and by never settling for the status quo. Keep pushing yourself, keep pushing your boundaries, and keep pushing the limits of what's possible.

Because in the world of business, it's not the strongest or the smartest who survives—it's the most innovative. And with innovation on your side, there's no limit to what you can achieve. Innovation isn't just a buzzword—it's the lifeblood of every successful entrepreneur. So, go ahead, unleash your creativity, and let innovation be your guide to success! The future is yours for the taking—innovate, adapt, and conquer!

Steve Jobs: Co-Founder of Apple Inc

Steve Jobs, the co-founder of Apple Inc., is renowned for his visionary approach to innovation, which has left an indelible mark on the technology industry. Throughout his tenure at Apple, Jobs demonstrated an unwavering commitment to pushing the boundaries of technology and design, leading to the creation of revolutionary products that have reshaped entire industries.

One of the most iconic examples of Jobs' embrace of innovation is the introduction of the iPhone. In 2007, Apple launched the first iPhone, a groundbreaking device that combined a phone, iPod, and internet communicator into a single sleek package. Jobs' vision for the iPhone revolutionized the way we communicate, work, and interact with technology, setting a new standard for smartphones and paving the way for the mobile revolution.

In addition to the iPhone, Jobs oversaw the development and launch of other groundbreaking products, including the iPad, MacBook Air, and Apple Watch. Each of these products exemplifies Jobs' commitment to innovation, as well as his keen understanding of consumer needs and desires. By anticipating market trends and embracing emerging technologies, Jobs positioned Apple as a leader in the tech industry and a pioneer of innovation.

Central to Jobs' approach to innovation was his ability to foster a culture of creativity and risk-taking at Apple. He encouraged his team to think differently and challenge the status quo, pushing them to explore innovative ideas and push the boundaries of what was possible. Jobs was known for his exacting standards and attention to detail, but he also recognized the importance of fostering a collaborative and supportive environment where innovation could flourish.

Jobs' visionary leadership and relentless pursuit of innovation have cemented Apple's position as a global leader in the tech industry. His legacy continues to inspire entrepreneurs and innovators around the world, reminding us of the transformative power of bold ideas and creative thinking. Through his example, Jobs has taught us that true innovation requires courage, vision, and a willingness to challenge convention.

NOTES AND KEY TAKEAWAYS

NOTES AND KEY TAKEAWAYS

Focus is the lens through which dramas become reality; adjust it with discipline, and watch your vision come into sharp focus.

CHAPTER 10: MAINTAINING FOCUS AND DISCIPLINE

In this chapter, we're diving into one of the key pillars of success: maintaining focus and discipline. In the whirlwind of entrepreneurial life, it's easy to get swept away by the tide of tasks, ideas, and distractions. But fear not! With the right strategies and mindset, you can stay on track and achieve your goals. Let's get started.

Lesson 28: Setting Clear Goals and Objectives

Imagine setting out on a journey without a map or destination in mind. Chances are, you'll end up lost or wandering aimlessly. The same principle applies to your entrepreneurial journey. Setting clear goals and objectives gives you direction and purpose.

Take some time to define what success looks like for you and your business. These goals should be specific, measurable, achievable, relevant, and time-bound (SMART).

Whether it's increasing revenue, expanding your customer base, or launching a new product, having clarity on your objectives will keep you focused and motivated.

Once you have your goals in place, break them down into smaller tasks and create a plan of action. Remember, clarity breeds focus.

Lesson 29: Developing Discipline in Execution

Setting goals is the first step but executing them is where the magic happens. This is where discipline comes into play. Discipline is about staying committed to your goals, even when the going gets tough. It means showing up every day and putting in the work, whether you feel like it or not. It's about making sacrifices and prioritizing what's truly important. So, how do you develop discipline?

Start by creating daily habits and routines that align with your goals.

Set aside dedicated time for focused work, eliminate distractions, and hold yourself accountable. Remember, consistency is key. Small actions repeated consistently over time lead to big results.

Celebrate your progress along the way, but don't lose sight of the bigger picture.

Lesson 30: Strategies for Maintaining Focus

In a world filled with notifications, emails, and endless to-do lists, maintaining focus can feel like a Herculean feat. But fear not, for there are strategies to help you reclaim your attention.

Start by identifying your most productive hours and dedicate them to your most important work. Consider implementing time-blocking techniques to allocate specific chunks of time to different tasks. Minimize multitasking—it's a productivity killer. Instead, practice single-tasking and give each task your undivided attention.

Embrace the power of prioritization. Not all tasks are created equal, so focus on the ones that align with your goals and values. Learn to say no to distractions that don't serve your purpose. And when your mind wanders (as it inevitably will), gently guide it back to the present moment. Mindfulness techniques such as deep breathing or short meditation breaks can help sharpen your focus and reduce mental clutter.

By setting clear goals, cultivating discipline, and implementing strategies to maintain focus, you'll steer your entrepreneurial ship through stormy seas with confidence and grace. Remember, resilience is not just about weathering the storms—it's about navigating them with purpose and determination. So, anchor yourself in focus, harness the power of discipline, and sail forth toward your entrepreneurial dreams. Smooth seas may not make skillful sailors, but with focus and discipline, you'll thrive amidst twists. Remember, Rome wasn't built in a day, and neither will your business. Stay disciplined, stay focused, and keep moving forward one step at a time. You've got this!

Mark Zuckerberg: CEO of Meta Platforms (formerly Facebook)

Mark Zuckerberg's journey with Facebook exemplifies the importance of maintaining focus and discipline in the face of myriad distractions and challenges. From its humble beginnings as a dorm room project to becoming a global social media behemoth, Facebook's success can be attributed in large part to Zuckerberg's unwavering commitment to his vision and his disciplined approach to execution.

Despite facing constant scrutiny, criticism, and external pressures, Zuckerberg remained steadfast in his mission to connect the world through social media. He possessed a laser focus on the long-term goals of the company, even as it encountered obstacles and setbacks along the way.

One key aspect of Zuckerberg's focus and discipline was his approach to product development. He prioritized the continuous improvement and innovation of Facebook's platform, ensuring that it remained relevant and engaging for users. Zuckerberg maintained a disciplined approach to rolling out new features and updates, carefully considering their impact on the user experience and the long-term trajectory of the company.

Additionally, Zuckerberg demonstrated discipline in his strategic decision-making, prioritizing long-term growth and sustainability over short-term gains. This was evident in Facebook's approach to acquisitions, where Zuckerberg carefully evaluated opportunities that aligned with the company's mission and strategic objectives. From the acquisition of Instagram to the purchase of WhatsApp, each move was made with a clear focus on enhancing Facebook's offerings and expanding its reach.

Overall, Mark Zuckerberg's ability to maintain focus and discipline amidst distractions and challenges was instrumental in driving the growth and success of Facebook. His unwavering commitment to his vision, combined with a disciplined approach to execution, allowed Facebook to navigate through rapid expansion and emerge as a dominant force in the world of social media.

NOTES AND KEY TAKEAWAYS

NOTES AND KEY TAKEAWAYS

Emotional intelligence is the silent force that steers the ship of entrepreneurship through turbulent seas with grace and resilience.

CHAPTER 11: CULTIVATING EMOTIONAL INTELLIGENCE

Emotions are like the fuel that powers our entrepreneurial journey. They can either propel us forward or bring us to a screeching halt. Emotional intelligence is the secret sauce that can elevate your entrepreneurial journey from surviving to thriving. It's not just about being smart or savvy; it's about understanding and managing emotions—yours and others.

Lesson 31: Understanding Emotions in Business

Ever found yourself in a whirlwind of emotions during a business meeting or when making a tough decision? Yeah, we've all been there. Understanding your emotions is like having a superpower in the business world.

Take a moment to recognize what you're feeling. Are you excited about a new opportunity? Nervous about a big presentation? Frustrated with setbacks? Acknowledging your emotions allows you to navigate them effectively.

Remember, emotions aren't your enemy—they're valuable messengers. They provide insights into your values, priorities, and areas needing attention. So, the next time you feel overwhelmed, pause, breathe, and listen to what your emotions are telling you.

Lesson 32: Practicing Empathy and Compassion

Entrepreneurship isn't just about numbers and strategies; it's about people—your team, customers, and partners. Empathy and compassion are your allies in building meaningful connections and fostering a positive work culture.

Put yourself in others' shoes. Understand their perspectives, challenges, and aspirations. When your team feels heard and understood, they become more engaged and motivated. And when customers feel valued, they become loyal advocates for your brand.

Compassion isn't just for others—it's for yourself too. Be kind to yourself amidst the ups and downs of entrepreneurship. Celebrate your wins, learn from your mistakes, and remember that you're doing the best you can.

Lesson 33: Managing Stress and Anxiety Effectively

Let's face it—entrepreneurship can be stressful. Deadlines, uncertainties, and the pressure to succeed can take a toll on your well-being. But here's the good news: you have the power to manage stress and anxiety effectively.

Find healthy coping mechanisms that work for you. Whether it's exercise, meditation, or spending time with loved ones, prioritize activities that recharge your batteries and bring you peace.

Break tasks into smaller, manageable chunks. When faced with overwhelming to-do lists, focus on one task at a time. Celebrate small victories along the way—they add up!

And don't be afraid to seek support when needed. Whether it's talking to a trusted friend, joining a support group, or seeking professional help, reaching out is a sign of strength, not weakness.

As entrepreneurs, we're often told to focus solely on the bottom line – to be rational, logical, and analytical. But in doing so, we sometimes forget about the human element of business – the emotions, the relationships, the empathy. Cultivating emotional intelligence isn't just about being a better leader or decision-maker; it's about being a better human being. So, take the time to understand your emotions, practice empathy and compassion, and manage stress and anxiety effectively. Your business – and your well-being – will thank you for it.

Oprah Winfrey: Media Mogul and Philanthropist

Oprah Winfrey's journey to becoming one of the most influential media figures of our time exemplifies the power of emotional intelligence in driving success. As a media mogul and philanthropist, Oprah has not only captured the hearts of millions but has also inspired positive change through her empathetic leadership style and authentic connections with her audience.

Oprah's ability to cultivate emotional intelligence played a pivotal role in her rise to prominence. She understood the importance of connecting with her audience on a deep emotional level, recognizing that genuine human connection is the cornerstone of effective communication. From the early days of her talk show, "The Oprah Winfrey Show," Oprah prioritized empathy and authenticity in her interactions with guests and viewers alike.

One of the hallmarks of Oprah's show was her ability to create a supportive and inclusive environment where guests felt safe to share their stories and vulnerabilities. Oprah listened attentively, showed genuine empathy, and offered words of encouragement and support. Her ability to empathize with others and create a space for open dialogue resonated with audiences around the world, fostering a sense of connection and belonging.

Moreover, Oprah's authenticity and vulnerability endeared her to her audience, making her relatable and trustworthy. She was not afraid to share her own struggles and triumphs, allowing viewers to see her as a flawed yet resilient human being. This transparency helped to break down barriers and build a deeper connection with her audience, fostering trust and loyalty over the years.

Beyond her talk show, Oprah's emotional intelligence has also guided her philanthropic endeavors and business ventures. She has used her platform to advocate for social justice, education, and empowerment, leveraging her influence to effect positive change in the world. Oprah's commitment to making a difference, stems from her deep empathy and compassion for others, driving her to use her resources and platform for the greater good.

In essence, Oprah Winfrey's success as a media mogul and philanthropist can be attributed in large part to her emotional intelligence. Her ability to connect with audiences on an emotional level, demonstrate empathy and authenticity, and leverage her influence for positive change has not only shaped her career but has also inspired millions around the world. Oprah's story serves as a powerful reminder of the transformative impact of emotional intelligence in leadership and communication.

NOTES AND KEY TAKEAWAYS

NOTES AND KEY TAKEAWAYS

Creativity is the spark that lights the fire of innovation; nurture it, and watch your ideas blaze a trail to success.

CHAPTER 12: HARNESSING CREATIVITY

Here, we're diving into the realm of creativity, a powerful tool in your entrepreneurial journey. Creativity isn't just about artistic flair; it's about finding new solutions, thinking outside the box, and innovating in ways that propel your business forward. So, let's explore how you can harness your creative energy to overcome challenges and seize opportunities.

Lesson 34: Stimulating Creative Thinking

Creativity often thrives in environments that encourage exploration and curiosity. As an entrepreneur, it's essential to create spaces—both physical and mental—that foster creative thinking. Take a step back from your daily routine, allow yourself to explore new ideas, and embrace unconventional perspectives.

Try brainstorming sessions with your team where no idea is too wild or outlandish. Remember, the craziest ideas sometimes lead to breakthrough innovations. And don't be afraid to experiment! Test out new approaches, even if they seem unconventional at first. Sometimes, the most unexpected combinations yield remarkable results.

Creativity is not just for artists or designers; it's a fundamental skill for entrepreneurs too. Think of creativity as a muscle that needs regular exercise to stay strong. Here are some simple exercises to stimulate your creative thinking:

- Mind Mapping: Start with a central idea or problem and branch out with related thoughts and associations. This visual technique can unlock new perspectives and connections.
- Brainstorming Sessions: Gather your team (or even just yourself) and brainstorm ideas without judgment. Quantity over quality at this stage. You never know which seemingly crazy idea might lead to a groundbreaking solution.

- Change Your Environment: Sometimes, a change of scenery is all it takes to get those creative juices flowing. Step away from your desk and explore new surroundings to spark fresh ideas.

Remember, creativity thrives in an environment of openness and exploration. Don't be afraid to think outside the box!

Lesson 35: Encouraging Innovation and Creativity

Innovation is the lifeblood of any successful business. But innovation doesn't happen in a vacuum—it requires a culture that values and nurtures creativity. Encourage your team to embrace innovation by celebrating their ideas, regardless of outcome.

Create platforms for sharing and collaboration, whether it's through regular brainstorming sessions, innovation challenges, or online forums. Encourage a diverse range of perspectives and voices within your team. Remember, innovation thrives when people from different backgrounds and experiences come together to solve problems.

And don't forget to lead by example. Show your team that you value creativity by exploring new ideas yourself and being open to feedback and suggestions.

Your enthusiasm for innovation will inspire others to think outside the box.

As an entrepreneur, it's essential to foster a culture of innovation within your team and organization. Here's how you can encourage creativity to flourish:

- Lead by Example: Show your team that you value and prioritize creativity by incorporating it into your own work and decision-making processes.
- Create a Safe Space: Encourage experimentation and risk-taking by creating a safe environment where failure is seen as a natural part of the learning process.
- Reward Creativity: Recognize and reward innovative ideas and efforts. Whether it's a shoutout in a team meeting or a small bonus, acknowledgment goes a long way in motivating creative thinking.

By nurturing a culture of innovation, you'll empower your team to think boldly and find novel solutions to challenges.

Lesson 36: Embracing Failure as Part of the Creative Process

Failure is an inevitable part of the creative process. But rather than seeing it as a setback, embrace failure as a learning opportunity. Every mistake, every misstep, is a chance to grow and improve.

Encourage a culture where failure is celebrated, not feared. Share stories of past failures and what you learned from them. Remind your team that failure is not the end—it's just a steppingstone on the path to success.

And remember, creativity thrives in an environment where people feel safe to take risks and make mistakes. Foster a culture of psychological safety, where people feel comfortable expressing themselves and sharing their ideas, knowing that they won't be ridiculed or punished for failure.

In conclusion, creativity is not just a trait; it's a skill that can be cultivated and nurtured over time. By stimulating creative thinking, encouraging innovation, and embracing failure as part of the process, you'll unleash your entrepreneurial potential and thrive amidst twists.

Now, go forth and unleash your creativity! The world is waiting for your innovative ideas and solutions.

Walt Disney: Founder of the Walt Disney Company

Walt Disney, the visionary founder of The Walt Disney Company, is renowned for his unparalleled creativity and innovative spirit, which revolutionized the entertainment industry and left an indelible mark on popular culture. Through his pioneering work in storytelling and animation, Disney transformed his dreams into reality, captivating audiences worldwide and establishing a legacy that continues to endure.

Disney's journey began with a bold vision to create a new form of entertainment that would captivate audiences of all ages. He believed in the power of storytelling to transport people to magical worlds and evoke deep emotions. With unwavering determination, Disney pushed the boundaries of traditional animation, pioneering techniques and technologies that would set the standard for the industry.

One of Disney's greatest strengths was his ability to dream big and think outside the box. He encouraged his team to push the limits of their imagination, challenging them to create characters and stories that would resonate with audiences on a profound level. From the iconic Mickey Mouse to beloved classics like Snow White and the Seven Dwarfs, Disney's characters became cultural icons, beloved by generations of fans around the world.

In addition to his creative genius, Disney was also a relentless innovator. He embraced modern technologies and techniques, constantly pushing the envelope to bring his visions to life. From the ground-breaking use of synchronized sound in Steamboat Willie to the revolutionary use of multiplane cameras in Snow White, Disney's innovations transformed the art of animation and set new standards for the industry.

But perhaps Disney's greatest legacy lies in his ability to inspire creativity and imagination in others. His timeless stories and characters continue to captivate audiences of all ages, sparking the imaginations of countless artists, writers, and filmmakers. Disney's influence can be seen in theme parks, movies, television shows, and even everyday products, demonstrating the enduring power of his creative vision.

In harnessing creativity, Walt Disney not only built a global entertainment empire but also created a legacy that continues to inspire and delight audiences around the world. His ability to dream big, push boundaries, and embrace innovation serves as a timeless example of the transformative power of creativity. As aspiring entrepreneurs, we can learn valuable lessons from Disney's legacy, remembering to embrace our own creativity and imagination as we pursue our dreams.

NOTES AND KEY TAKEAWAYS

Learning is the soil in which the seeds of entrepreneurship grow; cultivate it, and watch your potential blossom.

CHAPTER 13: CONTINUOUS LEARNING & GROWTH

Welcome to the exciting journey of continuous learning and growth! In this chapter, we'll explore three crucial lessons that are essential for entrepreneurial resilience: committing to lifelong learning, seeking feedback, and iterating, and embracing change as a catalyst for growth.

•

Lesson 37: Committing to Lifelong Learning

Entrepreneurship is a journey of constant evolution, and to stay ahead of the game, you must commit to lifelong learning. This doesn't mean pursuing formal education relentlessly, but rather embracing a mindset of curiosity and a willingness to learn from every experience. Whether it's reading books, attending workshops, or seeking out mentors, there are countless ways to expand your knowledge and skills. Remember, the more you learn, the better equipped you'll be to tackle any challenge that comes your way.

Picture this: your business is like a ship sailing through uncharted waters. To navigate successfully, you need a constantly updated map, right? That's where lifelong learning comes in. It's about being curious, staying hungry for knowledge, and constantly seeking new skills and insights.

Imagine if you stopped learning after you launched your business. You'd be like a plant without water, withering away in the sun. So, make a commitment to yourself today: no matter how busy you get, set aside time for learning. Whether it's reading books, taking online courses, attending workshops, or simply engaging in meaningful conversations, keep that learning flame burning bright.

Or imagine your business as a living organism. Just as a plant needs water and sunlight to thrive, your venture requires constant nourishment in the form of knowledge and learning. Committing to lifelong learning means staying curious and open to new ideas, trends, and technologies that can propel your business forward.

Think about it this way: every skill you acquire, every book you read, and every course you take is an investment in the future success of your business. Whether it's attending workshops, listening to podcasts, or networking with industry experts, never underestimate the power of learning to expand your horizons and unlock new opportunities.

Lesson 38: Seeking Feedback & Iterating

Feedback is a precious gift, albeit sometimes difficult to receive. But as an entrepreneur, feedback is your compass, guiding you toward improvement and growth. Actively seek feedback from your customers, your team members, and even your competitors. Listen attentively, without ego, and with a genuine desire to learn and evolve.

Use feedback as a tool for iteration. Take what resonates, discard what doesn't, and iterate upon your ideas, products, and strategies. Remember, every iteration is a step closer to perfection, and every failure is a lesson learned. Embrace the iterative process as a fundamental aspect of your entrepreneurial journey and watch as your resilience and adaptability soar.

Instead of fearing criticism, embrace it as a valuable tool for growth. Whether it's from customers, mentors, or peers, feedback provides insights into what's working well and what areas need improvement.

Remember, feedback is not a one-time event but an ongoing process. Make it a habit to solicit feedback regularly and be open to making iterations based on the insights you receive. By constantly refining your products, services, and strategies, you'll stay agile and responsive to the ever-changing needs of your market.

Take the feedback onboard, analyze it objectively, and use it to make informed decisions about your business. Remember, the path to success is paved with continuous improvement.

Lesson 39: Embracing Change as a Catalyst for Growth

Change is inevitable in the world of entrepreneurship, and rather than resisting it, you should embrace it as a catalyst for growth. Whether it's changes in technology, market trends, or consumer behavior, staying adaptable is key to staying ahead of the curve. Instead of viewing change as a threat, see it as an opportunity to innovate and evolve your business. Be proactive in identifying emerging trends and be willing to pivot when necessary. Remember, those who embrace change are the ones who thrive in the long run.

Think of change as a breath of fresh air for your business. It brings new ideas, new opportunities, and new perspectives.

But here's the catch: embracing change requires courage and flexibility. It means stepping out of your comfort zone, taking calculated risks, and trusting in your ability to adapt and thrive.

Stay agile, remain flexible, and be willing to pivot when necessary. Embrace change as a chance to challenge the status quo, disrupt industries, and carve out new paths to success. Remember, it's not the strongest or the smartest who survive, but those most adaptable to change.

Continuous learning and growth are the cornerstones of entrepreneurial resilience. By committing to lifelong learning, seeking feedback, and embracing change, you'll equip yourself with the tools and mindset needed to navigate the uncertainties of entrepreneurship with confidence and grace.

So, keep learning, keep iterating, and keep embracing change, because the journey toward success is an ever-evolving adventure!

Your journey towards resilience starts with a commitment to growth. So, keep an open mind, stay curious, and never stop striving for greatness.

Indra Nooyi: Former CEO of PepsiCo

Indra Nooyi's tenure as the CEO of PepsiCo stands as a testament to the vital role of continuous learning and growth in driving organizational success. Under her leadership, PepsiCo experienced significant expansion and transformation, thanks to her unwavering commitment to innovation, adaptability, and personal development.

Nooyi recognized early on that the consumer landscape was evolving rapidly, with shifting preferences towards healthier options and greater emphasis on sustainability. Instead of resting on the laurels of PepsiCo's existing product portfolio, she championed a strategic shift towards healthier alternatives and innovation. This included initiatives such as the "Performance with Purpose" agenda, which aimed to deliver sustained growth by focusing on healthier products, environmental sustainability, and empowering communities.

To execute this vision, Nooyi fostered a culture of continuous learning and growth within PepsiCo. She encouraged employees at all levels to embrace change, think creatively, and pursue personal and professional development. Nooyi herself led by example, constantly seeking new knowledge and insights to inform her decision-making and drive organizational progress.

Under her leadership, PepsiCo invested in employee training programs, leadership development initiatives, and cross-functional collaboration to nurture a culture of innovation and agility. Nooyi understood that in a fast-paced and competitive market, the ability to adapt and learn quickly was crucial for staying ahead of the curve.

Nooyi's commitment to continuous improvement not only led to financial success for PepsiCo but also fostered a sense of purpose and pride among employees. By encouraging a growth mindset and embracing change as an opportunity for learning and innovation, she empowered PepsiCo to navigate through challenges and capitalize on emerging trends effectively.

Today, PepsiCo's diverse product portfolio, which includes brands like Tropicana, Quaker, and Sabra, reflects Nooyi's legacy of innovation and adaptation. Her emphasis on continuous learning and growth has left an indelible mark on the company, shaping its culture and strategic direction for years to come. Indra Nooyi's leadership at PepsiCo serves as an inspiring example of how prioritizing continuous learning and growth can drive organizational success in a dynamic and ever-changing business environment.

NOTES AND KEY TAKEAWAYS

Resilient systems are the scaffolding that supports the structure of success; build them strong, and your business will weather any storm

CHAPTER 14: BUILDING RESILIENT SYSTEMS & PROCESSES

Welcome to the exciting journey of continuous learning and growth! In this chapter, we'll explore three crucial lessons that are essential for entrepreneurial resilience: committing to lifelong learning, seeking feedback, and iterating, and embracing change as a catalyst for growth.

Lesson 40: Streamlining Operations for Efficiency

Alright, let's talk about efficiency. We all want to get more done in less time, am I right? That's where streamlining operations comes into play. It's all about finding those little inefficiencies in your workflows and ironing them out.

Think about it like this: every minute you spend on a task that could be done faster or more effectively is a minute wasted. And in the world of entrepreneurship, time is precious. So, take a good look at your processes—whether it's your production line, your sales funnel, or your customer service—and ask yourself: "Is there a better way to do this?"

Maybe it's investing in new technology, maybe it's reorganizing your team's responsibilities, or maybe it's just getting rid of unnecessary steps. Whatever it is, the goal is simple: do more with less.

Picture this: you're running a marathon, but instead of lightweight running shoes, you're wearing heavy boots. Ouch, right? That's what it feels like when your business operations are clunky and inefficient. Streamlining your operations is like trading those boots for the perfect pair of running shoes. It's about removing unnecessary steps, automating wherever possible, and finding ways to do things smarter, not harder.

Ask yourself: Are there any bottlenecks in your workflow? Are there tasks that could be done more efficiently? Take the time to analyze your processes and identify areas for improvement. Trust me, your future self will thank you for it.

Take a moment to map out your workflows. Where are the bottlenecks?

Are there any steps that could be eliminated or simplified? Look for opportunities to automate repetitive tasks, delegate responsibilities, or invest in tools that can help you work smarter, not harder.

Remember, efficiency isn't just about saving time and money (although that's certainly a nice bonus). It's also about freeing up your mental bandwidth so you can focus on the things that truly matter, like growing your business and serving your customers.

Lesson 41: Creating Contingency Plans

Next up, let's talk about contingency plans. As much as we'd like to believe that everything will go according to plan, the reality is that life loves to throw us curveballs. That's why it's crucial to have backup plans in place for when things inevitably go sideways.

Start by identifying your most critical business functions. What would happen if your website crashed, or your supplier suddenly went out of business? By thinking through these scenarios ahead of time, you can develop contingency plans to keep your business afloat in times of crisis.

And remember, a good contingency plan isn't just a document collecting dust on a shelf. It's a living, breathing part of your business strategy that needs to be revisited and updated regularly.

So don't set it and forget it—keep those contingency plans fresh and relevant.

Ah, contingency plans—every entrepreneur's best friend (even if we sometimes forget to hang out with them). Picture this: you're cruising along, everything's going great, and then bam! A curveball comes out of nowhere and knocks you off course.

Now, you could panic, you could throw in the towel, or you could whip out that trusty contingency plan and keep on truckin'. Because here's the thing: setbacks are inevitable in business. But how you respond to them—that's what separates the resilient entrepreneurs from the rest.

So, take some time to think about the "what ifs." What if your supplier suddenly goes out of business? What if your website crashes during a big sale? What if a global pandemic shuts down the economy?

Okay, maybe that last one's a bit extreme, but you get the idea.

Life is unpredictable. No matter how well you plan, there's always a chance that things will go sideways. That's why it's essential to have contingency plans in place.

Having a contingency plan won't prevent bad things from happening, but it will help you bounce back quicker when they do.

Lesson 42: Automating Repetitive Tasks.

Raise your hand if you've ever felt like a hamster on a wheel, endlessly spinning through the same task's day after day. Yeah, we've all been there. But here's the good news - you don't have to keep doing things the hard way.

Automation is your best friend when it comes to tackling repetitive tasks.

From email marketing automation to customer relationship management systems, automation can be a game-changer for small businesses.

Look at your daily tasks. Are there any repetitive, time-consuming processes that could be automated? Maybe it's scheduling social media posts or sending out invoices. By harnessing the power of automation, you can free up valuable time and energy to focus on the bigger picture.

But remember, automation isn't a one-size-fits-all solution.

Be strategic about which tasks you choose to automate, and don't forget about the human touch. Sometimes, a personal email or phone call can go a long way in building relationships with your customers.

Remember, building resilient systems and processes isn't just about making your life easier (though that's a perk). It's about setting your business up for long-term success and sustainability. So, streamline those operations, craft those contingency plans, and automate those tasks like the resilient entrepreneur you are. You've got this!

Jack Ma: Co-founder of Alibaba Group

Jack Ma, the visionary co-founder of Alibaba Group, exemplifies the principles of building resilient systems and processes to propel a business to success. Through strategic investments and a forward-thinking approach, Ma transformed Alibaba into a global e-commerce powerhouse.

One of the key areas where Jack Ma focused his efforts was in technology infrastructure. Recognizing the critical role that technology plays in enabling e-commerce operations at scale, Ma made significant investments in building robust and scalable systems. Alibaba's platform was engineered to handle massive volumes of transactions, ensuring a seamless shopping experience for millions of users worldwide. By prioritizing the development of a reliable and efficient technological backbone, Ma laid the foundation for Alibaba's sustained growth and resilience.

In addition to technology infrastructure, Ma also placed a strong emphasis on logistics and supply chain management. He understood that efficient logistics were essential for delivering products to customers in a timely manner and maintaining a competitive edge in the e-commerce industry. Alibaba invested in building a network of warehouses, distribution centres, and transportation channels to streamline the flow of goods and optimize delivery processes. By optimizing logistics operations, Ma ensured that Alibaba could fulfil orders quickly and efficiently, even during periods of high demand or unforeseen disruptions.

Furthermore, Jack Ma was proactive in addressing risks and contingencies that could potentially impact Alibaba's operations. He implemented robust risk management processes to identify potential threats and vulnerabilities, allowing Alibaba to take pre-emptive action to mitigate risks and minimize the impact of disruptions. Ma also developed contingency plans to ensure business continuity in the event of unforeseen events such as natural disasters, regulatory changes, or cyber-attacks. By anticipating and preparing for potential challenges, Ma strengthened Alibaba's resilience and ability to adapt to changing circumstances.

Overall, Jack Ma's focus on building resilient systems and processes has been instrumental in Alibaba's success. Through strategic investments in technology infrastructure, logistics, and risk management, Ma ensured that Alibaba could withstand challenges and uncertainties while continuing to thrive and innovate in the dynamic e-commerce landscape. His visionary leadership and commitment to building resilience have established Alibaba as a global leader in online retail, inspiring entrepreneurs around the world to prioritize the development of robust systems and processes in their own businesses.

NOTES AND KEY TAKEAWAYS

Mindfulness is the anchor that keeps entrepreneurs grounded amidst the whirlwind of business; tether yourself to it and find peace in every moment.

CHAPTER 15: MINDFULNESS

Picture this: a bustling office, phones ringing, emails flooding in, deadlines looming large. Amidst this chaos, how can we maintain our calm and navigate through the twists and turns of entrepreneurship?

Now Picture this: you're in the midst of a storm, but instead of getting swept away, you're standing strong, rooted in the present moment. That's the magic of mindfulness.

Lesson 43: Practicing Mindfulness in Business

Let's start by understanding what mindfulness truly means. It's about being present in the moment, fully engaged in what you're doing without judgment. In the fast-paced world of business, it's easy to get caught up in worries about the future or regrets about the past. But by practicing mindfulness, we can train our minds to focus on the present moment, enhancing our decision-making abilities and reducing stress.

Imagine sitting in a meeting with a potential investor. Instead of letting your mind wander about what might go wrong or what you should have said differently in a previous meeting, bring your attention back to the present. Listen actively, observe body language, and respond thoughtfully. This simple act of mindfulness can make a world of difference in how you navigate business interactions.

Or Picture this: You're in the middle of a hectic day, emails flooding in, meetings back-to-back, and deadlines looming over your head. Sound familiar? In the chaos of entrepreneurship, it's easy to get swept away by the frenzy of activity. But here's the thing – amidst the chaos, there's an oasis of calm waiting for you: mindfulness.

Mindfulness in business is about bringing your full attention to the present moment. It's about being fully engaged in what you're doing, whether it's tackling a challenging task or having a conversation with a client. By practicing mindfulness, you can cultivate clarity, focus, and a sense of calm amidst the storm.

Try this: Take a few moments each day to pause, breathe, and ground yourself in the present moment. Notice the sensations in your body, the thoughts passing through your mind, and the emotions you're experiencing.

By anchoring yourself in the present, you can navigate the ups and downs of entrepreneurship with greater ease and resilience. So, how can you integrate mindfulness into your daily routine? It could be as simple as taking a few minutes each day to meditate, going for a mindful walk during your lunch break, or even just pausing to take a few deep breaths before responding to a challenging email. The key is to find what works for you and make it a regular practice.

Lesson 44: Developing Resilience through Meditation

Meditation is like a superpower for entrepreneurs. It's a practice that can help you build resilience, cultivate emotional intelligence, and tap into your inner strength. Whether you're dealing with stress, uncertainty, or self-doubt, meditation can be a powerful tool for navigating the challenges of entrepreneurship.

You don't need to be a meditation guru to reap the benefits. Even just a few minutes of meditation each day can make a world of difference. Find a quiet space, sit comfortably, and focus on your breath. Notice the sensations of each inhale and exhale, and whenever your mind wanders (which it inevitably will), gently bring it back to the breath.

As you continue to practice meditation, you'll develop greater clarity, resilience, and a sense of inner peace. So, carve out some time each day to nurture your mind and soul through the practice of meditation. Your business – and your well-being – will thank you for it.

Lesson 45: Finding Balance through Mindful Practices.

Entrepreneurship is a marathon, not a sprint. And like any endurance race, finding balance is key to staying in the game for the long haul. But here's the catch – balance isn't just about juggling work and personal life; it's about finding harmony in all areas of your life.

Mindful practices can help you find that balance by fostering self-awareness, self-care, and self-compassion. Whether it's going for a walk-in nature, practicing yoga, or enjoying a leisurely meal with loved ones, find what brings you joy and nourishes your soul.

Remember, you're not just a business owner – you're a human being with hopes, dreams, and a beating heart. So, prioritize your well-being, honor your needs, and cultivate a sense of balance in your life. By doing so, you'll not only thrive in business but in life as well.

Ray Dalio: Founder of Bridgewater Associates

Ray Dalio, the founder of Bridgewater Associates, exemplifies how cultivating resilience through mindfulness can profoundly impact success in finance and investment management. His journey is a testament to the power of mindfulness in navigating the complexities of the financial world with clarity and equanimity.

At the core of Dalio's approach is his "Principles" framework, which he developed to guide decision-making and foster a culture of radical transparency and open-mindedness within Bridgewater Associates. This framework emphasizes the importance of continuous improvement and learning from both successes and failures.

Mindfulness plays a significant role in Dalio's life and leadership style. He practices meditation and engages in regular self-reflection, which allows him to maintain a clear and focused mindset even in the face of uncertainty and volatility in the markets. By cultivating mindfulness, Dalio is able to approach challenges with a sense of calm and perspective, enabling him to make sound decisions and adapt to changing circumstances effectively.

Dalio's commitment to mindfulness not only contributes to his success in finance but also enhances his overall well-being and personal fulfilment. By prioritizing mindfulness, he is able to maintain balance in his life and avoid the pitfalls of stress and burnout that are all too common in the high-pressure world of finance.

In essence, Ray Dalio's story serves as a compelling case study on how mindfulness can be a powerful tool for cultivating resilience, both professionally and personally. By integrating mindfulness practices into his life and leadership approach, Dalio has not only achieved financial success but also found greater fulfilment and peace of mind along the way.

NOTES AND KEY TAKEAWAYS

NOTES AND KEY TAKEAWAYS

Leadership is not about commanding from the front; it's about inspiring resilience from within and guiding your team through the darkest nights towards the brightest dawn

CHAPTER 16: LEADING WITH RESILIENCE

As an entrepreneur, you're not just charting your own course but also guiding others through the stormy seas of business. It's a big responsibility, but fear not, because we're here to equip you with the tools you need to lead with resilience, inspire your team, and foster a culture of strength and perseverance.

Lesson 46: Leading by Example

You've probably heard the phrase "lead by example" countless times, but what does it really mean? Well, it's about walking the talk. As a leader, your actions speak louder than words. If you want your team to embody resilience, you need to demonstrate it yourself.

Think about the leaders who have inspired you in your journey. What did they do differently? Chances are, they led by example. They didn't just talk the talk; they walked the walk. As an entrepreneur, your actions speak louder than words. Your team looks up to you, so lead with integrity, passion, and determination. Show them what resilience looks like in action. You've probably heard the phrase "lead by example" countless times, but what does it really mean?

Well, it's about walking the talk. As a leader, your actions speak louder than words. If you want your team to embody resilience, you need to demonstrate it yourself.

Think about the leaders who have inspired you in your journey. What did they do differently? Chances are, they led by example. They didn't just talk the talk; they walked the walk. As an entrepreneur, your actions speak louder than words. Your team looks up to you, so lead with integrity, passion, and determination. Show them what resilience looks like in action.

Picture this: you're the captain of a ship navigating through stormy seas. Your crew looks to you for guidance and reassurance. In entrepreneurship, it's no different. Your team will take cues from how you handle adversity and uncertainty.

Leading by example means embodying the resilience you want to see in your team. It's about staying calm under pressure, embracing change with open arms, and showing unwavering determination in the face of challenges. When your team sees you facing obstacles head-on and emerging stronger, they'll be inspired to do the same.

Think about how you handle challenges and setbacks. Do you stay calm under pressure? Do you approach problems with a solution-focused mindset? Your team is watching, and they'll take cues from your behavior. So, be the kind of leader you'd want to follow.

Lesson 47: Inspiring and Motivating Others

As a leader, one of your most important roles is to inspire and motivate your team. When times get tough, your words and actions can make all the difference. Take the time to uplift and encourage your team members, reminding them of their strengths and capabilities.

As an entrepreneur, you're not just a manager; you're a motivator-in-chief. Your team relies on you to keep their spirits high, especially during tough times. So, how do you inspire and motivate others?

Start by sharing your vision. Help your team understand the bigger picture and how their contributions fit into it. Celebrate wins, no matter how small, and acknowledge their hard work. Encourage creativity and innovation by fostering an environment where ideas are welcomed and appreciated. Remember, a motivated team is a resilient team.

Leading isn't just about telling people what to do; it's about inspiring them to do their best work. Take the time to understand what motivates each member of your team. Is it recognition, autonomy, or a sense of purpose? Whatever it is, find ways to tap into it and unleash their full potential. Celebrate their successes, provide constructive feedback, and always be their biggest cheerleader.

Share stories of resilience and triumph, both within your organization and from other successful entrepreneurs. Celebrate small wins along the way and remind your team of the bigger picture and the impact of their work. A motivated team is a resilient team, ready to tackle any challenge that comes their way.

And don't forget to lead with optimism. Even when things seem bleak, maintain a positive outlook, and instill confidence in your team. Your attitude can be contagious, so spread positivity wherever you go.

Lesson 48: Fostering a Culture of Resilience Within your Team.

Ever heard the phrase, "Teamwork makes the dream work"? Well, it's true! Building a resilient team starts with fostering a culture of resilience. How do you do that?

Firstly, encourage open communication. Create a safe space where team members feel comfortable sharing their thoughts and concerns. Be transparent about challenges and involve your team in problem-solving.

Secondly, promote collaboration and support. Encourage your team to help each other out and help when needed. Remember, we're all in this together.

Lastly, celebrate resilience. Recognize and reward team members who demonstrate resilience in the face of adversity. By highlighting examples of resilience, you're reinforcing its importance within your team culture.

Building a resilient team starts with creating a supportive and empowering culture. Your team members should feel safe to take risks, make mistakes, and learn from failure.

Encourage open communication and collaboration. Create an environment where everyone feels valued and heard. Celebrate successes together and learn from failures as a team. Emphasize the importance of adaptability and flexibility and empower your team to embrace change with confidence.

Culture is the glue that holds your team together, and resilience should be at its core. Create an environment where failure is viewed as a learning opportunity, not a setback. Encourage open communication and transparency, so team members feel comfortable sharing their struggles and seeking support.

Building a resilient team starts with creating a supportive and empowering culture. Your team members should feel safe to take risks, make mistakes, and learn from failure.

Encourage open communication and collaboration. Create an environment where everyone feels valued and heard. Celebrate successes together and learn from failures as a team. Emphasize the importance of adaptability and flexibility and empower your team to embrace change with confidence.

Remember, leadership is not about having all the answers; it's about empowering others to find solutions.

So, go ahead, lead with courage, lead with heart, and lead with resilience. Your team is counting on you, and together, you'll thrive amidst the twists of entrepreneurship.

Mary Barra: CEO of General Motors

Mary Barra's tenure as the CEO of General Motors (GM) stands as a beacon of resilience amidst adversity in the automotive industry. Assuming leadership during a turbulent period marked by recalls and regulatory scrutiny, Barra faced formidable challenges head-on.

Upon taking the helm, Barra orchestrated a remarkable culture transformation within GM. Recognizing the critical need to restore trust and confidence, she prioritized safety, quality, and innovation as cornerstones of the company's ethos. Under her stewardship, GM adopted a proactive approach to address safety concerns, implementing rigorous quality control measures and fostering a culture of accountability and transparency.

Barra's leadership style epitomized resilience in action. She navigated GM through a series of crises with unwavering resolve and poise, earning respect and admiration from employees, investors, and customers alike. Her transparent communication and decisive actions instilled confidence in GM's ability to weather the storm and emerge stronger than before.

Amidst the challenges, Barra remained steadfast in her commitment to driving GM's turnaround and resurgence. She championed initiatives to innovate and adapt to changing market dynamics, positioning GM as a leader in electric and autonomous vehicles. Her strategic vision and forward-thinking approach propelled GM's transformation into a nimble and innovative powerhouse in the automotive industry.

Ultimately, Mary Barra's leadership exemplifies resilience in its purest form. By leading with integrity, empathy, and unwavering determination, she not only steered GM through adversity but also inspired a culture of resilience and innovation that continues to fuel the company's success. Her legacy serves as a testament to the transformative power of resilient leadership in overcoming challenges and achieving sustainable growth.

NOTES AND KEY TAKEAWAYS

Gratitude is the currency of success; spend it generously, and watch your blessings multiply.

CHAPTER 17: CELEBRATING SUCCESS & GRATITUDE

Congratulations! You've made it to the final chapter of our journey together. As entrepreneurs, we often get so caught up in the hustle and bustle of running our businesses that we forget to take a step back and appreciate how far we've come. Now, it's time to take a moment to pause, reflect, and celebrate your journey. In this chapter, we'll delve into the importance of celebrating success and practicing gratitude in our entrepreneurial journey.

Lesson 49: Recognizing and Celebrating Achievements

It's time to put on your party hat and break out the confetti because we're diving into the wonderful world of recognizing and celebrating achievements.

Picture this: You've been grinding away at your entrepreneurial endeavors, pouring your heart and soul into every project, overcoming hurdles left and right, and making strides toward your goals. It's been a journey filled with ups and downs, late nights, and early mornings. But through it all, you've persevered, and now, it's time to shine a spotlight on your accomplishments.

Recognizing and celebrating achievements isn't just about patting yourself on the back (although that's certainly part of it).

It's about acknowledging the hard work, dedication, and resilience that have brought you to this point. It's about taking a moment to bask in the glow of success, to revel in the fruits of your labor, and to share that joy with those who have supported you along the way.

So, how do you go about recognizing and celebrating achievements in your entrepreneurial journey? Let's break it down:

- Acknowledge the Wins: Whether it's closing a big deal, launching a new product, or hitting a milestone, take the time to acknowledge and celebrate every win, no matter how small. Each achievement is a steppingstone on your path to success, and it deserves to be recognized.

- Share the Success: Your achievements are not yours alone—they belong to your team, your partners, your supporters, and anyone else who has contributed to your success. So, don't be shy about sharing the spotlight. Celebrate as a team, acknowledge everyone's contributions, and let them know that their hard work has not gone unnoticed.
- Reflect and Appreciate: Take a moment to reflect on the journey that led to this achievement. Think about the challenges you faced, the lessons you learned, and the growth you've experienced along the way. And don't forget to express gratitude for the opportunities, the support, and the blessings that have made it all possible.
- Celebrate in Style: Whether it's a team lunch, a champagne toast, or a virtual dance party, find a way to celebrate your achievements in style. Get creative, have fun, and let loose. After all, you've earned it!
- Remember, celebrating achievements isn't just a nice-to-have—it's an essential part of building a positive and resilient culture within your organization. So, don't wait for the big wins to roll in before you break out the party hats. Celebrate every step of the way, and watch as your team grows stronger, more motivated, and more resilient than ever before. Cheers to your success!

Lesson 50: Practicing Gratitude Daily

Imagine waking up each morning with a heart full of gratitude, ready to take on the day's challenges with a renewed sense of purpose and joy. This is the power of practicing gratitude daily. It's not just about saying "thank you" occasionally; it's about cultivating a mindset of appreciation that permeates every aspect of your life, including your entrepreneurial journey.

In the fast-paced world of entrepreneurship, it's easy to get swept away by the pressures, demands, and setbacks that come your way. But amidst the chaos, practicing gratitude can be a beacon of light, guiding you through the ups and downs with resilience and grace. So, what does practicing gratitude daily entail?

1. Gratitude Journaling: Start your day by writing down three things you're grateful for. They could be as simple as the sunshine streaming through your window, the supportive team members you work with, or the opportunity to pursue your passion through entrepreneurship. By acknowledging and documenting these blessings, you set a positive tone for the day ahead.
2. Expressing Appreciation: Take the time to thank those around you who contribute to your journey—your team members, mentors, clients, and loved ones. Whether it's a heartfelt note, a

kind gesture, or a simple "thank you," expressing appreciation fosters deeper connections and strengthens relationships, both personally and professionally.

3. Finding Gratitude in Challenges: Even in the face of adversity, there are silver linings to be found. Instead of dwelling on setbacks, look for the lessons, growth opportunities, and unexpected blessings that emerge from challenges. Perhaps a failed project teaches you resilience, a difficult client interaction helps you improve your communication skills, or a setback redirects you toward a more promising path. By reframing challenges as opportunities for growth and learning, you cultivate resilience and gratitude in the face of adversity.
4. Mindful Moments of Gratitude: Throughout the day, pause for mindful moments of gratitude. Whether it's savoring a cup of coffee, taking a walk-in nature, or simply breathing deeply, allow yourself to fully experience and appreciate the present moment. These moments of mindfulness not only ground you in the here and now but also deepen your sense of gratitude for the abundance that surrounds you.
5. Counting Your Blessings: Before you go to bed each night, take a moment to reflect on the day and count your blessings. What moments brought you joy, inspiration, or a sense of fulfillment? By ending your day with a gratitude practice, you cultivate a sense of peace, contentment, and optimism that carries over into the next day.

Incorporating these simple yet powerful practices into your daily routine can transform your mindset, attitude, and outlook on life. As you cultivate a habit of gratitude, you'll find yourself navigating the entrepreneurial journey with resilience, optimism, and a deep sense of fulfillment. So, take a moment to pause, breathe, and give thanks for the blessings that surround you. Gratitude truly is the key to thriving amidst twists and turning your entrepreneurial dreams into reality.

Richard Branson: Founder of Virgin Group

Richard Branson, the charismatic founder of the Virgin Group, has built an empire spanning numerous industries, including music, airlines, telecommunications, and space travel. Throughout his entrepreneurial journey, Branson has cultivated a culture of celebration and gratitude that has become synonymous with the Virgin brand.

One of Branson's key leadership traits is his unwavering appreciation for the contributions of his team. He understands that success is a collective effort and goes out of his way to acknowledge the hard work and dedication of his employees. Whether it's through bonuses, recognition programs, or simply a heartfelt thank-you, Branson ensures that his team feels valued and appreciated.

Moreover, Branson extends his gratitude beyond the confines of his company to include customers, stakeholders, and the broader community. He understands the importance of building strong relationships with customers and goes above and beyond to exceed their expectations. Whether it's providing exceptional customer service or launching innovative products and services, Branson consistently expresses his gratitude to customers for their support and loyalty.

Branson's leadership style is characterized by humility, authenticity, and a sense of fun. He leads by example, showing genuine appreciation for the people around him and creating a positive and inclusive work environment. Branson's approachability and willingness to listen to others make him highly relatable to both employees and customers alike.

At the heart of Branson's success is his ability to celebrate achievements with genuine gratitude. Whether it's a milestone reached, a successful product launch, or a record-breaking year, Branson takes the time to reflect on the accomplishments and express his gratitude to everyone who played a part. This culture of celebration and gratitude has not only fostered loyalty and goodwill within the Virgin Group but has also attracted top talent and inspired innovation.

In summary, Richard Branson's entrepreneurial journey serves as a shining example of the power of celebrating success with gratitude. By acknowledging the contributions of his team, expressing gratitude to customers and stakeholders, and fostering a culture of positivity and appreciation, Branson has built a legacy of enduring success with the Virgin Group.

NOTES AND KEY TAKEAWAYS

NOTES AND KEY TAKEAWAYS

CONCLUSION

Congratulations on completing "Thriving Amidst Twists: 50 Essential Lessons for Entrepreneurial Resilience"! You've embarked on a journey to strengthen your resilience and fortify your entrepreneurial spirit, and now it's time to reflect on the lessons learned and chart your course forward with confidence.

As entrepreneurs, we often find ourselves navigating through twists, turns, and unexpected challenges. But through these challenges, we can grow, adapt, and emerge stronger than ever before. Throughout this book, we've explored essential strategies and insights to help you thrive amidst the twists of entrepreneurship. Let's take a moment to revisit some key takeaways and remind ourselves of the fundamental principles that will guide us on our entrepreneurial journey:

1. Embrace Change: Change is inevitable, and embracing it is the first step towards resilience. Remember to stay flexible, adapt to new circumstances, and seize opportunities that arise from change.
2. Learn from Failure: Failure is not the end; it's a steppingstone to success. Embrace failure as a valuable learning experience and use it to fuel your growth and innovation.
3. Build a Support Network: Surround yourself with mentors, peers, and advisors who can offer guidance, support, and encouragement during challenging times. Remember, you don't have to go it alone.
4. Prioritize Self-Care: Your well-being is paramount to your success as an entrepreneur. Make time for self-care, prioritize your mental and physical health, and find balance in your personal and professional life.
5. Persist with Purpose: Stay committed to your goals and vision, even when faced with obstacles and setbacks. Persistence and determination are key ingredients for entrepreneurial success.
6. Make Strategic Decisions: Approach decision-making with clarity, foresight, and a willingness to take calculated risks. Trust your instincts,

but also seek input from trusted advisors and mentors.

7. Manage Finances Wisely: Maintain a healthy financial foundation for your business by managing cash flow effectively, diversifying revenue streams, and planning for the unexpected.
8. Foster a Resilient Team: Cultivate a culture of resilience within your team, encourage open communication, and provide support and encouragement to your team members during challenging times.
9. Embrace Innovation: Stay ahead of the curve by embracing innovation, creativity, and continuous improvement. Be willing to experiment, adapt, and innovate to meet the evolving needs of your customers.
10. Practice Gratitude: Take time to celebrate your successes, express gratitude for your accomplishments, and acknowledge the support of those who have helped you along the way.

As you continue your entrepreneurial journey, remember that resilience is not a destination but a lifelong practice. It requires patience, perseverance, and a willingness to learn and grow from every experience. So, embrace the twists, turns, and challenges that come your way, and let them propel you towards greater resilience, success, and fulfillment.

Thank you for joining me on this journey of discovery and growth. May you continue to thrive amidst the twists of entrepreneurship and achieve your wildest dreams.

Here's to your resilience, your courage, and your boundless potential.

Keep thriving!

Sumegha Mehta Borar

NOTES AND KEY TAKEAWAYS

NOTES AND KEY TAKEAWAYS

www.ingramcontent.com/pod-product-compliance
Lightning Source LLC
Chambersburg PA
CBHW020438220526
45464CB00002B/763
9798322271949